The Modern Spirituality Series

Henri Nouwen

The Modern Spirituality Series

Metropolitan Anthony of Sourozh

Henri Nouwen

Lionel Blue

John Main

Thomas Merton

Carlo Carretto

Michael Ramsey

Jean Vanier

Dietrich Bonhoeffer

Bede Griffiths

Henri Nouwen

Introduced and edited by
John Garvey

TEMPLEGATE PUBLISHERS

First published in 1988 by
Darton, Longman and Todd Ltd
89 Lillie Road, London SW6 1UD

© 1988 Henri J. M. Nouwen

Introduction and arrangement
© 1988 John Garvey

ISBN 0-87243-169-X

First published in the United States in 1988 by

Templegate Publishers
302 E. Adams St./P.O. Box 5152
Springfield, Illinois 62705

The cover photograph of René Magritte's
"The Tempest" is reproduced
with the permission of the Wadsworth Atheneum,
Hartford, Connecticut. Bequest of Kay Sage Tanguy.

Cover Design: Scott Turner

Contents

Acknowledgements

Thanks are due to Ave Maria Press for permission to use extracts from *Behold the Beauty of the Lord*, *In Memoriam*, *Love in a Fearful Land* and *With Open Hands*; Doubleday & Co. from *Compassion*, *Lifesigns*, *Clowning in Rome*, *The Genesee Diary*, *A Cry for Mercy* and *The Wounded Healer*; Harper & Row from *¡Gracias!*, *A Letter of Consolation*, *Making All Things New* and *The Way of the Heart*.

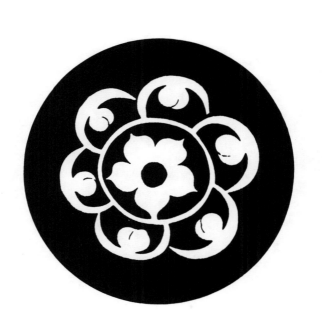

Introduction

Henri J. M. Nouwen was born on 24 January 1932, in Nijkerk, Holland. In 1957 he was ordained as a priest for the Archdiocese of Utrecht, and studied psychology at the Catholic University of Nijmegen. After receiving his degree in 1964 he travelled to the United States. He worked in America for four years, first as a fellow in the Program for Religion and Psychiatry at the Menninger Clinic in Topeka, Kansas, then as a visiting professor in the Psychology Department at the University of Notre Dame. In 1968 he returned to Holland, taught at the Pastoral Institute in Amsterdam and at the Catholic Theological Institute in Utrecht, and received a theology degree from the University of Nijmegen.

In 1971 he returned to the United States and taught pastoral theology at Yale Divinity School until 1981. During this time he served as a fellow at the Ecumenical Institute in Collegeville, Minnesota and a scholar in residence at the North American College in Rome. In 1974 and 1978 he spent several months in the Abbey of the Genesee, a Cistercian monastery in Piffard, New York, where he was allowed to live and work as a monk. In 1981 and 1982 he visited Latin America, spending much of his time in poor communities. From 1983 to 1985 he taught at Harvard Divinity School. In 1985 he travelled to France, where he lived for nine months at L'Arche, a Christian community founded by Jean Vanier in which people with handicaps and their assistants try to live together in the spirit of the Gospel. Since 1986 Nouwen has been priest-in-residence at Daybreak, a L'Arche community in Toronto.

Henri Nouwen has a wide and varied audience. His books and articles have influenced readers from a number of religious traditions, and speak with a directness which is rare in spiritual writing. He is a Roman Catholic priest who has spent most of his time as a teacher in divinity schools founded to serve Protestant churches, and whose writings – drawing as they often have on the traditions of Eastern Orthodoxy – are listed in Orthodox book catalogues. Although Nouwen was trained as a psychologist and took another degree in theology, his work is refreshingly free from jargon of any sort. He has dealt with current issues and events, without becoming merely trendy; he has drawn on the most ancient Christian traditions, but is able to speak of them, and from them, in a totally modern fashion.

In 1978 Nouwen was interviewed by Todd Brennan for *The Critic*, a Catholic journal published in Chicago. He told Brennan: 'I have always used as my prime resource some of my own observations and my own personal struggles with whatever I am writing about. This is because I have always believed that one of the main objectives of ministry is to make your own faith struggles available to others, to articulate for others your own doubts, and to say, in effect, "I don't know the answers either. I am simply a catalyst, simply somebody who wants to articulate for you things that you already know but might get a better grip on if there are some words for them." '

This may explain part of Nouwen's appeal. Much spiritual writing, classic as well as modern, too often seems to have been handed down from an Olympian height, or to have been composed by someone quite unlike the reader. Nouwen's writing is, as he suggested in the *Critic* interview, very personal. The personal is, of course, always at the heart of any good spiritual writing. Whether one reads St John of the Cross or Metropolitan Anthony Bloom, it is clear that what is being described has in some way been experienced; but this experience ordinarily must be read as it were between the lines. What appeals to so many people about the work of Henri Nouwen is that he speaks directly of the struggle which is alluded to in a second-hand way in much spiritual writing. Another central feature of his work is that he makes it clear, in a direct and personal way, that the spiritual life is at many times a matter of struggle, failure and discouragement. We advance as we learn how to fall and rise, and still keep going. I am reminded here of what one Orthodox monk answered when someone asked: 'What do you monks *do* in the monastery?' His answer was: 'Fall and get up again, fall and get up again, fall and get up again.'

This would be a discouraging answer if it were not for the fact that the process also involves times of great encouragement, joy and hope. Nouwen has tried consistently to describe all of it – the uncertainty and doubt, as well as the joy and peace. I know a woman who had followed

Nouwen's work for years; she was shocked at the weaknesses he confessed in *Genesee Diary*, an account of the several months he spent at a Trappist monastery, where he was allowed to live and work as a monk. Like many people, she preferred her spiritual guides to be (or at least to seem) infallible and serene, and not bothered, distracted or irritable; that was too much the way she herself was, much of the time. Further reflection made it clear to her that this is what made the book helpful, rather than scandalous. It is good to know that knowledge is won at a price; and self-understanding is almost never a painless process of learning the lessons by rote, applying them and then moving on. It may disturb some people to find a man whose writing has been helpful to them confessing impatience, discouragement, and anger at petty things; it may disturb them that a man who has written about prayer says in his journal that he finds himself restless and distracted.

But the truly disturbing thing would be if he never were distracted, never encountered his own anger or pettiness, never found himself discouraged. How on earth could writing which emerged from such an unrealistically detached and pure plane help any of us? We find it much more interesting that Jacob wrestled with an angel than we would if Scripture told us that an angel had wrestled with an angel. Too much writing which concerns the life of prayer has assumed a superior vantage point on the part of the writer, and too many readers have welcomed the distance. It is an important aspect of Henri Nouwen's writing that he has eliminated it.

There are risks here, of course. Writing about one's personal struggles can turn into a subtle form of narcissism, and too intimate a discussion of one's spiritual state can be as embarrassing to anyone outside of the penitent/confessor relationship as an open discussion of one's sex life. Nouwen, however, writes of these things in a manner which is clearly not meant to present us with an image of the interestingly tormented spiritual seeker; he is not afraid to look foolish or petty, and readers who, all of them, have been foolish or petty at times may find it encouraging to know that this is part of the spiritual struggle. Narcissism in spirituality emphasizes interesting and dramatic sins, and wonderfully dramatic revelations. In Nouwen's work we often find something much more modest, and therefore more true and helpful. In such works as *Genesee Diary* and *¡Gracias!*, his day-to-day reflections – sometimes pedestrian and occasionally obvious, and at other times profound and striking – make it clear to the reader that spirituality is a matter of dailiness, a matter of trying to refer *all* aspects of our lives to God, including the undramatic, the petty, the routine. This is very much in keeping with Nouwen's understanding of ministry, but it is more than an applied theory. In offering all the stuff of daily life as the material we work on, with God's help, he reveals something too easily forgotten: ours is an incarnational religion. Because the Word became flesh, everything human is the proper concern of the Christian, including the most mundane moments – the delight we take in the smell of fresh bread, or the disappointment

15

we know when an expected letter fails to arrive. A practical and helpful emphasis on this attentiveness to God's work at the level of dailiness is certainly one of the elements which has made Nouwen a popular writer.

This is not to say that he pays attention only to ordinary dailiness. In *Compassion, ¡Gracias!* and *Love in a Fearful Land*, Nouwen deals directly with those larger issues which involve Christians, individually and in community, in the struggle for social justice. Nouwen has spent time with the people who are at the centre of 'liberation theology', and not only with them . . . he has seen the places which make it seem so necessary to the people at the centre of that movement. It would be easy to see a contradiction between this concern and the desire for a new appreciation of the contemplative life, which took Nouwen to a Trappist monastery for several months.

The idea that there is a contradiction here, however, is a surrender to an essentially secular understanding of life, which makes a clear distinction between the political and public realm on the one hand, and the private, personal realm on the other; the latter is the place to which spirituality has been consigned.

There are twin impulses at work in Christian thinking these days. One would claim that the area of social morality, too often ignored in the Church's definition of its role, is in fact the place where we must now concentrate our collective attention. The other impulse is to ignore or reject the social as a distraction from the needs of the individual soul, which is saved or damned inde-

16

pendently of the social concerns which seem pressing in a particular political climate.

One service the writings of Henri Nouwen might perform for us is to reveal how false this division is. His writing is very much in the spirit of the Epistle of St James, who asks: 'What causes conflicts and quarrels among you? Do they not spring from the aggressiveness of your bodily desires? You want something which you cannot have, and so you are bent on murder; you are envious, and cannot attain your ambition, and so you quarrel and fight . . .' (4:1–2, NEB). Personal and social morality are not two separate things, and can never be in a religion which is serious about the belief that the Word became flesh, with all of the individual and social meanings which halo us because we are flesh and blood, living in community as well as in solitude, dying alone, while we are at the same time loved and remembered by others.

The attempt to make two essentially different things of personal and social morality is a by-product of secular thinking, which would relegate all of religion to the realm of the secular. And secularity is, according to Orthodox theologian Alexander Schmemann, 'a lie about the world'. The Christian lives in a world informed by one of Jesus' most disturbing statements: what you have done to the least of these, you have done to me. That is at the base of our relationship to one another, at the personal as well as the political level, and where it is not at the base we need to repent, and start again. This is why there is no contradiction between the Henri Nouwen who writes about the use of icons in prayer, and the Henri Nouwen who writes about the need for justice in Central America.

It must be said, however, that Nouwen's concern with justice is never primarily political, or determined by merely pragmatic considerations. He has pointed out the need for a spirituality which can deal with the defeat of the hopes of the poor, the failure of peace efforts, a spirituality which can continue to hope when all worldly reasons for hope have been lost. The accusation brought against some advocates of liberation theology is that they measure Christianity against socialist ideology, and trim their religion to fit an ideological model; this has never been true of Nouwen's writing. He is a thoroughly orthodox Christian, and it is his fervent orthodoxy which has brought him to social concerns.

In the past several years Nouwen's writing has appeared occasionally in an interesting American magazine, *New Oxford Review*, and it seems to me that this is a natural place for it. The magazine was founded by an Anglican layman who converted to Roman Catholicism. Its politics can be roughly described as progressive, and its theology as conservative; the magazine, founded while the editor was an Anglican, took its name from the Oxford Movement. In some journal entries which have appeared there, Nouwen has deplored the increasingly secular atmosphere of his native Holland, the vanishing of appreciation for the observance of those daily and seasonal rituals which unite generations and keep communities in touch with the Church and with one another. His work has also appeared in *Sojourners*, a magazine issued by a Washington D.C.-based community of evangelical Protestants who emphasize a biblical approach to political issues. This often leads them to social activism, a direction very different from that of the religious right, which is very influential in American evangelical circles. I once asked Nouwen about his involvement with this community, and he said that when he spoke to them what they wanted to hear about was not politics, but prayer.

In all of Henri Nouwen's work there is a sense of eagerness, a curiosity, a hunger to see the ways in which the Holy Spirit moves people in our time; and it is not bound either by the sort of traditionalism which fears anything new, on the one hand, or by a slavish concern for the spirit of the age on the other. Not all of Nouwen's readers or friends agree with him at every point, and his work has covered many points indeed. What they find throughout his work is an understanding that the will of God must be attended to in all aspects of life, even those which sometimes seem routine, and that it has to do with serving one another. This service is undertaken — or refused — at every level: family, the religious community, and the world which those of us who are comfortable too often exclude from our consciousness: the world of the poor, the handicapped, all of those people who make us uncomfortable and who seem so inconvenient. Henri Nouwen's writing has brought this world to the attention of many who might not otherwise have been able to see it, not through any unique hard-heartedness of their own, but through a common human insensitivity which Nouwen shares with us and reveals in his writings as he struggles against it, and as he moves into a new understanding of what we are called to do and be. This form of spiritual writing is often helpful in the most practical ways. It is a welcome alternative to the forms of preaching too often encountered by people who need something better – the bland recommendation of prayer, usually offered with no practical advice on what prayer means, with little sense that real prayer is a matter of life and death, and involves a daily, usually not very glamorous, struggle.

Here I must be personal. I am not at all objective about Henri Nouwen. I have known him for years, since the time he taught at the University of Notre Dame and I studied there. I first knew him as a good preacher, whose Masses I attended because the sermons would almost certainly be worth hearing. Then, through mutual friends, my wife and I and, later, our children came to know him through shared dinners, visits to our home, and – when the group of our friends who were centred at Notre Dame dispersed – through letters. We have been each other's guest, which is a pleasant way to know someone. We had known one another for years before I read one of his books, and when I did I recognized the voice. Some things do not quite come through the way they do in the flesh: a passionate and sometimes restless nature, an eagerness to understand and be understood, an attentiveness to the person with whom he is talking. It was interesting to watch him try to cross the Yale Divinity School yard, as one student or professor after another stopped him to talk about the many projects they were involved in together. At the end of the day, he was exhausted; it was easy to see why.

At Notre Dame he grew close to many people; it was important to him to understand what was happening among students in the volatile atmosphere of the American sixties, but he was interested in other things as well – drama, art, good films. This interest was not a desire to be current, but to understand what is at work beneath the surface of the times, and that desire has led to a refreshed understanding of ancient Christian tradition. It does not surprise many people who knew him then that Henri would go on to write books about living among the poor in Latin America and meetings with Liberation theologians, or, for that matter, that he would write about the Fathers and Mothers of the Desert, and time spent in a monastery, and the help icons can offer us when we pray. The ability to show that the traditions of ancient and contemporary Eastern Christianity are of direct practical help to us, and are as new as the Gospel itself, is one of Henri Nouwen's most important contributions. Henri Nouwen's work has been and continues to be helpful to many, and if this book – which I hope will be helpful in its own right – leads others to turn to Nouwen's books, as well as to the authors who enrich his own writing, it will have done its work.

JOHN GARVEY

Questioning the false self

Which questions guide our lives? Which questions do we make our own? Which questions deserve our undivided attention and full personal commitment? Finding the right questions is as crucial as finding the right answers.

Why do we children of light so easily become conspirators with the darkness? The answer is quite simple. Our identity, our sense of self, is at stake. Secularity is a way of being dependent on the responses of our milieu.

The secular or false self is the self which is fabricated, as Thomas Merton says, by social compulsions. 'Compulsive' is indeed the best adjective for the false self. It points to the need for ongoing and increasing affirmation. Who am I? I am the one who is liked, praised, admired, disliked, hated, or despised.

Unlimited love

O Lord, look with favor on us, your people, and impart your love to us – not as an idea or concept, but as a lived experience. We can only love each other because you have loved us first. Let us know that first love so that we can see all human love as a reflection of a greater love, a love without conditions or limitations.

If I can recognize you in the Sacrament of the Eucharist, I must be able to recognize you in the many hungry men, women and children. If I cannot translate my faith in your presence under the appearance of bread and wine into action for the world, I am still an unbeliever.

Silence and inner pilgrimage

Abba Tithoes once said, 'Pilgrimage means that a man should control his tongue.' The expression 'To be on pilgrimage is to be silent' . . . expresses the conviction of the Desert Fathers that silence is the best anticipation of the future world. The most frequent argument for silence is simply that words lead to sin.

. . . Let us at least recognize how often we come out of a conversation, a discussion, a social gathering, or a business meeting, with a bad taste in our mouth. How seldom have long talks proved to be good and fruitful? Would not many if not most of the words we use be better left unspoken?

A second, more positive meaning of silence is that it protects the inner fire. Silence guards the inner heat of religious emotions. This inner heat is the life of the Holy Spirit within us. Thus, silence is the discipline by which the inner fire of God is tended and kept alive.

The mystery of silence

The third way that silence reveals itself as the mystery of the future world is by teaching us to speak. A word with power is a word which comes out of silence.

A word that bears fruit is a word that emerges from the silence and returns to it. It is a word that reminds us of the silence from which it comes and leads us back to that silence. A word that is not rooted in silence is a weak, powerless word that sounds like a 'clashing cymbal or a booming gong' (1 Corinthians 13:1).

Thus silence is the mystery of the future world. It keeps us pilgrims and prevents us from becoming entangled in the cares of this age. It guards the fire of the Holy Spirit who dwells within us. It allows us to speak a word that participates in the creative and recreative power of God's own Word.

Prayer and vulnerability

Our many prayers are in fact confessions of our inability to pray. But they are confessions that enable us to perceive the merciful presence of God.

It is indeed through our broken, vulnerable, mortal ways of being that the healing power of the eternal God becomes visible to us. Therefore we are called each day to present to our Lord the whole of our lives – our joys as well as our sorrows, our successes as well as our failures, our hopes as well as our fears.

Gratitude and action

Whether they confront evil in the world or support the good, disciplined actions are always characterized by gratitude.

To persevere without visible success we need a spirit of gratitude. An angry action is born of the experience of being hurt; a grateful action is born of the experience of healing. Angry actions want to take; grateful actions want to share. Gratitude is the mode of action undertaken as part of the discipline of patience.

The compassionate life is a grateful life, and actions born out of gratefulness are not compulsive but free, not somber but joyful, not fanatical but liberating. When gratitude is the source of our actions, our giving becomes receiving, and those to whom we minister become our ministers because in the center of our cares for others we sense a caring presence, and in the midst of our efforts we sense an encouraging support.

God's servanthood

... It is not said of Jesus that he reached down from on high to pull us up from slavery, but that he became a slave with us. God's compassion is a compassion that reveals itself in servanthood. Jesus became subject to the same powers and influences that dominate us, and suffered our fears, uncertainties and anxieties with us.

'Being as we are, he was humbler yet, even to accepting death, death on a cross.' Here the essence of God's compassion is announced ... In this humiliation, Jesus lived out the full implications of emptying himself to be with us in compassion ... It was a death that we 'normal' human beings would hardly be willing to consider ours.

In the Gospel stories of Jesus' healings, we sense how close God wants to be with those who suffer. But now we see the price God is willing to pay for this intimacy. It is the price of ultimate servanthood, the price of becoming a slave, completely dependent on strange, cruel, alien forces. We spontaneously protest against this road of self-emptying and humiliation. We certainly appreciate people who try to understand us. We are even grateful for people who want to feel with us. But we become suspicious when someone chooses to undergo the pain that we would avoid at all costs. We understand conditional solidarity, but we do not understand solidarity that has no limits.

A *downward pull*

Jesus' compassion is characterized by a downward pull. That is what disturbs us. We cannot even think about ourselves in terms other than those of an upward pull, an upward mobility in which we strive for better lives, higher salaries and more prestigious positions. Thus, we are deeply disturbed by a God who embodies a downward movement... Here we see what compassion means. It is not a bending toward the underprivileged from a privileged position; it is not a reaching out from on high to those who are less fortunate below; it is not a gesture of sympathy or pity for those who fail to make it in the upward pull. On the contrary, compassion means going directly to those people and places where suffering is most acute and building a home there. God's compassion is total, absolute, unconditional, without reservation... It is the compassion of a God who does not merely act as a servant, but whose servanthood is a direct expression of his divinity.

The great mystery of God's compassion is that in his compassion, in his entering with us into the condition of a slave, he reveals himself to us as God... His self-emptying and humiliation are not a step away from his true nature... Rather, in the emptied and humbled Christ we encounter God, we see who God really is, we come to know his true divinity.

Discipleship and discernment

. . . It is clear that prayer is not an effort to make contact with God, to bring him to our side. Prayer, as a discipline that strengthens and deepens discipleship, is the effort to remove everything that might prevent the Spirit of God, given to us by Jesus Christ, from speaking freely to us and in us. The discipline of prayer is the discipline by which we liberate the Spirit of God from entanglement in our impatient impulses. It is the way we allow God's Spirit to move where he wants.

This indicates that prayer as a discipline of patience is the human effort to allow the Holy Spirit to do his re-creating work in us. This discipline involves many things. It involves the constant choice not to run from the present moment in the naïve hope that salvation will appear around the next corner. It involves the determination to listen carefully to people and events so as to discern the movements of the Spirit. It involves the ongoing struggle to prevent our minds and hearts from becoming cluttered with the many distractions that clamor for our attention. But above all, it involves the decision to set aside time every day to be alone with God and listen to the Spirit.

Praying for our enemies

The first thing we are called to do when we think of others as our enemies is to pray for them. This is certainly not easy. It requires discipline to allow those who hate us or those toward whom we have hostile feelings to come into the intimate center of our hearts.

Yet every time we overcome this impatience with our opponents and are willing to listen to the cry of those who persecute us, we will recognize them as brothers and sisters too. Praying for our enemies is therefore a real event, the event of reconciliation. It is impossible to lift our enemies up in the presence of God and at the same time continue to hate them. Seen in the place of prayer, even the unprincipled dictator and the vicious torturer can no longer appear as the object of fear, hatred and revenge, because when we pray for them we stand at the center of the great mystery of Divine Compassion.

There is probably no prayer as powerful as the prayer for our enemies. But it is also the most difficult prayer since it is most contrary to our impulses. This explains why some saints consider prayer for our enemies the main criterion of holiness.

Prayer and martyrdom

Prayer and martyrdom are intimately connected. When the early Christians were no longer required to become martyrs, that is, witnesses for the Lord with their blood, many became 'confessors', witnesses through a life of unceasing prayer.

To cry out to the God of life in the midst of darkness, to hold on to joy while walking in a valley of tears, to keep speaking of peace when sounds of war fill the air – that is what prayer is about. It is indeed a clinging to the Lord when all is being torn apart by greed, hatred, violence and war.

In its pure form, prayer is the divine breath of those whom the world tries to suffocate with terror. Prayer is the martyrdom of those who live.

The struggle to pray

Our inclination is to show our Lord only what we feel comfortable with. But the more we dare to reveal our whole trembling self to him, the more we will be able to sense that his love, which is perfect love, casts out all our fears.

Therefore, Lord, I promise I will not run away, not give up, not stop praying, even when it all seems useless, pointless, and a waste of time and effort. I want to let you know that I love you even though I do not feel loved by you, and that I hope in you even though I often experience despair. Let this be a little dying I can do with you and for you as a way of experiencing some solidarity with the millions in this world who suffer far more than I do.

Prayer and work

I came to the monastery to learn to live in the presence of God, to taste him here and now, but there is so much 'ego-climbing' going on within me. I have so many ideas I want to write about, so many books I want to read, so many skills I want to learn . . . and so many things I want to say to others now or later, that I do not SEE that God is all around me and that I am always trying to see what is ahead, overlooking him who is so close.

I'd better start thinking a little more about my attitude toward work. If I have learned anything this week, it is that there is a contemplative way of working that is more important for me than praying, reading, or singing. Most people think that you go to the monastery to pray. Well, I prayed more this week than before but also discovered that I have not learned yet to make the work of my hands into a prayer.

. . . I had just begun to realize how much my own life was motivated by self-glory: even going to a monastery could be a form of self-indulgence. My problem with work is obviously related to my tendency to look at manual labor as a necessary job to earn a couple of free hours to do my own work. Even when this work seems very spiritual, such as reading about prayer, I often look at it more as an opportunity to make interesting notes for future lectures or books than as a way to praise the Lord.

Creating a free space

This afternoon I worked a few hours alone in the river carrying heavy granite rocks to the bank and making piles. While doing this, I realized how difficult 'nepsis' – the control of thoughts – really is. My thoughts not only wandered in all directions, but started to brood on many negative feelings, feelings of hostility toward people who received more than I, feelings of self-pity in regard to people who had not written, and many feelings of regret and guilt toward people with whom I had strained relationships. While pulling and pushing with the crowbar, all these feelings kept pulling and pushing in me . . .

My reading about the spirituality of the Desert has made me aware of the importance of 'nepsis'. Nepsis means mental sobriety, spiritual attention directed to God, watchfulness in keeping the bad thoughts away, and creating free space for prayer. While working with the rocks I repeated a few times the famous words of the old Desert Fathers: '*Fuge, tace et quiesce*' ('live in solitude, silence and inner peace'), but only God knows how far I am, not only from this reality but even from this desire.

Once in a while I cursed when the rock was too heavy . . . I tried to convert my curse into a prayer . . . but nothing spectacular happened . . . When I walked home I realized that it was exactly the lack of spiritual attention that caused the heaviness in my heart.

Attachment

Somewhere during these weeks I read that sadness is the result of attachment. Detached people are not the easy victims of good or bad events in their surroundings and can experience a certain sense of equilibrium. I have the feeling that this is an important realization for me. When my manual work does not interest me, I become bored, then quickly irritated and sometimes even angry, telling myself that I am wasting my time. When I read a book that fascinates me, I become so involved that the time runs fast, people seem friendly, my stay here worthwhile, and everything one big happy event.

Of course both 'moods' are manifestations of false attachments and show how far I am from any healthy form of indifference.

But if prayer were my only concern, all these . . . laudable things could be received as free gifts. Now, however, I am obsessed by these desires which are false, not in themselves, but by their being in the wrong place in the hierarchy of values. That, I guess, is the cause of my moodiness. For the time being it seems important to be at least aware of it.

Learning to live on the other side

I am beginning to discover the 'other world' in which I live. When I run, monks smile; when I work very intensely, they make signs to slow down; and when I worry, I know it is usually useless. Last week I asked John Eudes how he thought I was doing. He said, 'I guess OK. Nobody has mentioned you yet.' That would not be a good sign everywhere! I really must enter that 'other side', the quiet, rhythmic, solid side of life, the deep solid stream moving underneath the restless waves of my sea.

Father Marcellus read a story about Beethoven during dinner. When Beethoven had played a new sonata for a friend, the friend asked him after the last note, 'What does it mean?' Beethoven returned to the piano, played the whole sonata again and said, 'That is what it means.' This type of response seems the only possible response to the question, 'What does the contemplative life mean?'

Anger

Anger is indeed one of the main obstacles of the spiritual life. Evagrius writes: 'The state of prayer can be aptly described as a habitual state of imperturbable calm.' The longer I am here, the more I sense how anger bars my way to God.

Being in a monastery like this helps me to see how the anger is really mine. In other situations there are often enough 'good reasons' for being angry, for thinking that others are insensitive, egocentric or harsh, and in those circumstances my mind easily finds anchor points for its hostility. But here! People couldn't be nicer, more gentle, more considerate. They really are very kind, compassionate people. That leaves little room for projection. In fact, none. It is not *he* or *they*, but it is simply *me*. I am the source of my own anger and no one else. I am here because I want to be here, and no one forces me to do anything I do not want to do. If I am angry and morose, I now have a perfect chance to look at its source, its deepest roots.

Exploring the inner life

In the contemplative life every conflict, inner or outer, small or large, can be seen as the tip of an iceberg, the expressive part of something deeper and larger. It is worthwhile, even necessary, to explore that which is underneath the surface of our daily actions, thoughts and feelings . . .

. . . Two ideas are clear. First: Do not run away from your inner feelings even when they seem fearful. By following them through you will understand them better and be more free to look for new ways when the old ways run into a blank wall. Second: When you explore in depth your unruly and wild emotions you will be confronted with your sinful self. This confrontation should not lead to despair but should set you free to receive the compassion of God without whom no healing is possible.

Self and community

... I discover *myself* in a new way in the love of God. St Bernard of Clairvaux describes as the highest degree of love the love of ourselves for God's sake.

... It is not only ourselves we discover in our individuality but our fellow human beings as well, because it is God's glory itself that manifests itself in his people in an abundant variety of forms and styles. The uniqueness of our neighbors is not related to those idiosyncratic qualities that only they and nobody else have, but it is related to the fact that God's eternal beauty and love become visible in these unique, irreplaceable, finite human beings. It is exactly in the preciousness of the individual person that the eternal love of God is refracted and becomes the basis of a community of love.

The guestmaster, Father Francis, showed me a letter of gratitude written by the leader of a group of retarded boys who visited the monastery ... Vespers had impressed them the most ... I think that often those who are poor at verbal communication sense better the mood and atmosphere of a place or an event than very cerebral, 'discussing' types. These retarded boys had sensed the mystery hidden under the meanings of the words.

Writing about prayer

Writing about prayer is often very painful since it makes you so aware of how far away you are from the ideal you write about . . . This week all I am reading and writing about is prayer. I am so busy with it and often so excited about it that I have no time left to pray, and when I pray, I feel more drawn to my ideas on prayer than to praying.

While it is true that in order to pray you have to empty your heart and mind for God, you also have to empty your heart and mind of your feelings and ideas on prayer. Otherwise, prayer gets in the way of praying.

I have a strong feeling that my intellectual formation is just as much a hindrance as a help to prayer. It is hard not to desire good insights during prayer and not to fall into a long inner discussion with myself. Every time some kind of insight comes to me, I find myself wondering how I can use it in a lecture, a sermon, or an article, and very soon I am far away from God and all wrapped up in my own preoccupations. Maybe this is what makes the Jesus Prayer so good for me. Simply saying, 'Lord Jesus Christ, have mercy on me' a hundred times, a thousand times, ten thousand times, as the Russian peasant did, might slowly clean my mind and give God a little chance.

Looking back

One of the experiences of prayer is that it seems that nothing happens. But when you stay with it and look back over a long period of prayer, you suddenly realize that something has happened. What is most close, most intimate, most present, often cannot be experienced directly but only with a certain distance. When I think that I am only distracted, just wasting my time, something is happening too immediate for knowing, under-standing and experiencing. Only in retrospect do I realize that something very important has taken place. Isn't this true of all really important events in life? When I am together with someone I love very much, we seldom talk about our relationship. The relationship, in fact, is too central to be a subject of talk. But later, after we have separated and write letters, we realize how much it all meant to us . . .

I wonder if in this sense I am not participating in what the apostles experienced. When Jesus was with them, they could not fully realize or under-stand what was happening. Only after he had left did they sense, feel and understand how close he really had been to them. Their experience after the resurrection became the basis for their expectation.

The inner self

Today I imagined my inner self as a place crowded with pins and needles. How could I receive anyone in my prayer when there is no real place for them to be free and relaxed? When I am still so full of preoccupations, jealousies, angry feelings, anyone who enters will get hurt. I had a very vivid realization that I must create some free space in my innermost self so that I may indeed invite others to enter and be healed. To pray for others means to offer others a hospitable place where I can really listen to their needs and pains. Compassion, therefore, calls for a self-scrutiny that can lead to inner gentleness.

If I could have a gentle 'interiority' – a heart of flesh and not of stone, a room with some spots on which one might walk barefooted – then God and my fellow humans could meet each other there. Then the center of my heart can become the place where God can hear the prayer for my neighbors and embrace them with his love.

Christic and humility

Christ is King and therefore his will and not mine should be the ultimate criterion of my actions. Enough to start feeling very uncomfortable. But today in the liturgy as well as during my meditation, I started to see and feel that Christ became our King by obedience and humility. His crown is a crown of thorns, his throne is a cross.

The hard reality is that in our world humility and obedience are never totally separated from power and manipulation: we are challenged to see the will of God in people who are sinful like ourselves and always subject to using their authority more for the worldly kingdom, even when called Church, than for the Kingdom of Christ. But Jesus allowed the will of his Father to be done through Pilate, Herod, mocking soldiers, and a gaping crowd that did not understand. How little is asked of me. I am asked only to obey people who share my love for Christ and have often had a greater share in his suffering than I have.

But let me at least realize today that if I am ever asked to accept or exercise authority over others, it should be an authority based on a sharing in the suffering of those whom I ask to obey.

Christian leadership

Christian leadership is acquired only through service. This service requires the willingness to enter into a situation, with all the human vulnerabilities we have to share with our fellow beings. This is a painful and self-denying experience, but an experience which can indeed lead us out of our prisons of confusion and fear. Indeed, the paradox of Christian leadership is that the way out is the way in, that only by entering into communion with human suffering can relief be found.

. . . All Christians are constantly invited to overcome their neighbors' fear by entering into it with them, and to find in the fellowship of suffering a way to freedom.

Loneliness

We live in a society in which loneliness has become one of the most painful human wounds. The growing competition and rivalry which pervade our lives from birth have created in us an acute awareness of our isolation. This awareness has in turn left many with a heightened anxiety and an intense search for the experience of unity and community. It has also led people to ask anew how love, friendship, brotherhood and sisterhood can free them from isolation and offer them a sense of intimacy and belonging. All around us we see the many ways by which the people of the western world are trying to escape this loneliness . . .

But the more I think about loneliness, the more I think that the wound of loneliness is like the Grand Canyon – a deep incision in the surface of our existence which has become an inexhaustible source of beauty and self-understanding.

Loneliness as a gift

Therefore I would like to voice loudly and clearly what might seem unpopular and maybe even disturbing: The Christian way of life does not take away our loneliness; it protects and cherishes it as a precious gift. Sometimes it seems as if we do everything possible to avoid the painful confrontation with our basic human loneliness, and allow ourselves to be trapped by false gods promising immediate satisfaction and quick relief.

But perhaps the painful awareness of loneliness is an invitation to transcend our limitations and look beyond the boundaries of our existence. The awareness of loneliness reveals to us an inner emptiness that can be destructive when misunderstood, but filled with promise for those who can tolerate its sweet pain.

Loneliness and others

When we are impatient, when we want to give up our loneliness and try to overcome the separation and incompleteness we feel, too soon, we easily relate to our human world with devastating expectations. We ignore what we already know with a deep-seated, intuitive knowledge – that no love or friendship, no intimate embrace or tender kiss, no community, commune, or collective, no man or woman, will ever be able to satisfy our desire to be released from our lonely condition.

Many marriages are ruined because neither partner was able to fulfill the often hidden hope that the other would take his or her loneliness away. And many celibates live with the naïve dream that in the intimacy of marriage their loneliness will be taken away.

When the minister lives with these false expectations and illusions he prevents himself from claiming his own loneliness as a source of human understanding, and is unable to offer any real service to the many who do not understand their own suffering.

This morning Father John explained to me that the killdeer is a bird that fools you by simulating injury to pull your attention away from her eggs which she lays openly on a sandy place. Beautiful! Neurosis as weapon? How often I have asked pity for a very unreal problem in order to pull people's attention away from what I didn't want them to see.

Shared suffering

How can wounds become a source of healing? This is a question which requires careful consideration. For when we want to put our wounded selves in the service of others, we must consider the relationship between our professional and personal lives.

On the one hand, no minister can keep his own experience of life hidden from those he wants to help . . . On the other hand, it would be very easy to misuse the concept of the wounded healer by defending a form of spiritual exhibitionism. A minister who talks in the pulpit about his own personal problems is of no help to his congregation, for no suffering human being is helped by someone who tells him that he has the same problems. Remarks such as, 'Don't worry, because I suffer from the same depression, confusion and anxiety as you do,' help no one. This spiritual exhibitionism adds little faith to little faith and creates narrow-mindedness instead of new perspectives. Open wounds stink and do not heal.

Making one's own wounds a source of healing . . . does not call for a sharing of superficial personal pains but for a constant willingness to see one's own pain and suffering as rising from the depth of the human condition which all people share.

The service of suffering

Perhaps the main task of the minister is to prevent people from suffering for the wrong reasons. Many people suffer because of the false supposition on which they have based their lives. That supposition is that there should be no fear or loneliness, no confusion or doubt. But these sufferings can only be dealt with creatively when they are understood as wounds integral to our human condition. Therefore ministry is a very confronting service. It does not allow people to live with illusions of immortality and wholeness. It keeps reminding others that they are mortal and broken, but also that with the recognition of this condition, wholeness starts.

A Christian community is therefore a healing community not because wounds are cured and pains are alleviated, but because wounds and pains become openings or occasions for a new vision. Mutual confession then becomes a mutual deepening of hope, and sharing weakness becomes a reminder to one and all of the coming strength.

Healing and liberation

When loneliness is among the chief wounds of the minister, hospitality can convert that wound into a source of healing. Concentration prevents the minister from burdening others with his pain and allows him to accept his wounds as helpful teachers of his own and his neighbor's condition. Community arises where the sharing of pain takes place, not as a stifling form of self-complaint, but as a recognition of God's saving promises.

Our loneliness and isolation have become so much a part of our daily experience, that we cry out for a liberator who will take us away from our misery and bring us justice and peace.

To announce, however, that the Liberator is sitting among the poor and that the wounds are signs of hope and that today is the day of liberation, is a step very few can take. But this is exactly the announcement of the wounded healer: 'The Master is coming – not tomorrow, but today, not next year, but this year, not after all our misery has passed, but in the middle of it, not in another place but right here where we are standing.'

The fear of silence

We know there is some connection between prayer and silence, but if we think about silence in our life it seems that it isn't always peaceful; silence can also be frightening.

. . . There are two silences; one is frightening and the other is peaceful. For many, silence is threatening. They don't know what to do with it. If they leave the noise of the city behind and come upon a place where no cars are roaring, no ships are tooting, no trains rumbling, where there is no hum of radio or television, where no records or tapes are playing, they feel their entire body gripped by an intense unrest. They feel like a fish which has been set on dry land. They have lost their bearings. There are some students who can't study without a solid wall of music surrounding them. If they are forced to sit in a room without that constant flow of sound, they grow very nervous.

Thus, for many of us, silence has become a real disturbance. There was a time when silence was normal and a lot of racket disturbed us. But today, noise is the normal fare, and silence, strange as it may seem, has become the real disturbance. It is not hard to understand, therefore, that people who experience silence in this way will have difficulty with prayer.

Prayer of little faith

Often . . . prayer of petition is treated with a certain disdain. Sometimes we regard it as less than prayer of thanksgiving and certainly less than prayer of praise. Prayer of petition is supposedly more egocentric . . .

But the question is whether this distinction helps us understand what prayer is. The important thing about prayer is not whether it is classified as petition, thanksgiving or praise, but whether it is prayer of hope or of little faith.

The prayer of little faith is where you hold fast to the concrete of the present situation in order to win a certain security. The prayer of little faith is filled with wishes which beg for immediate fulfillment. This prayer of wish fulfillment has a Santa Claus naïveté which wants to satisfy specific desires. When the prayer is not heard, that is, when you don't get the present you wanted, there is disappointment, even hard feelings and bitterness . . . The man of little faith prays a prayer that is carefully reckoned, even stingy, and which is upset by every risk. There is no danger of despair and no chance for hope.

Prayer of hope

Those with hope do not get tangled up with concerns of how their wishes will be fulfilled. So, too, their prayers are not directed toward the gift, but toward the one who gives it. Their prayers might still contain just as many desires, but ultimately it is not a question of having a wish come true but of expressing an unlimited faith in the giver of all good things . . .

Hope is based on the premise that the other gives only what is good. Hope includes an openness by which you wait for the other to make his loving promise come true, even though you never know when, where or how this might happen.

The person who prays with hope might still ask for many things; he or she might ask for everything, and very concretely, like nice weather or an advancement. This concreteness is even a sign of authenticity. For if you ask only for faith, hope, love, freedom, happiness, modesty, humility, etc., without making them concrete . . . you probably haven't really involved God in your real life. But if you pray in hope, all those concrete requests are merely ways of expressing your unlimited trust in him who fulfills all his promises, who holds out for you nothing but good, and who wants for himself nothing more than to share his goodness with you.

Dependence and openness

If we say that it's good to turn to God in prayer for a spare minute, or if we grant that a person with a problem does well to take refuge in prayer, we have as much as admitted that praying is on the margin of life and that it doesn't really matter.

Whenever you feel that a little praying can't do any harm, you will find that it can't do much good either. Prayer has meaning only if it is necessary and indispensable. Prayer is prayer only when we say that without it, a person could not live.

Those who look prayerfully on the world are those who do not expect happiness from themselves, but who look forward toward the other who is coming. It is often said that those who pray are conscious of their dependence, and in their prayer they express their helplessness. This can easily be misunderstood. The praying person not only says, 'I can't do it and I don't understand it,' but also, 'Of myself, I don't have to be able to do it, and of myself, I don't have to understand it.' When you stop at that first phrase, you often pray in confusion and despair, but when you can also add the second, you feel your dependence no longer as helplessness but as a happy openness which looks forward to being renewed.

The God of all

Conversion to God, therefore, means a simultaneous conversion to the other persons who live with you on this earth. The farmer, the worker, the student, the prisoner, the sick, the black man, the white man, the weak, the strong, the oppressed and the oppressor, the patient and the one who heals, the tortured and the torturer, the boss and the flunkey, not only are they people like you, but they are also called to make themselves heard and to give God a chance to be the God of all.

. . . You are Christian only so long as you look forward to a new world, so long as you constantly pose critical questions to the society you live in, so long as you emphasize the need of conversion both for yourself and for the world, so long as you in no way let yourself become established in a situation of seeming calm, so long as you stay unsatisfied with the *status quo* and keep saying that a new world is yet to come. You are Christian only when you believe that you have a role to play in the realization of this new Kingdom, and when you urge everyone you meet with a holy unrest to make haste so that the promise might soon be fulfilled.

The depths of the ordinary

It is indeed in the usual, normal and ordinary events that we touch the mystery of human life. When a child is born, a man and woman embrace, or a mother or father dies, the mystery of life reveals itself to us. It is precisely in the moments when we are most human, most in touch with what binds us together, that we discover the hidden depths of life.

Could it be that I had applied oil on my own mother to help her prepare for the final battle? Is it not possible that she who lived her life in such close union with God had also come to know the power of the Evil One more intimately than many others? Is it inconceivable that she who had spent so many hours in prayer was also most aware of the one whom we call 'the Tempter'? Is it not possible that great faith reveals the possibility of doubt, that great love reveals the possibility of hate and that great hope reveals the possibility of despair?

Three weeks before her death she said to me, 'I am afraid to die; not to go to the hospital, not to undergo surgery, not to suffer pain: I am afraid to appear before God and show him my life.' It was this great encounter that frightened her. She was so deeply impressed by God's awesome greatness and had become so aware of her own nothingness that the great encounter could only frighten her.

Christian death

Why do we think that Christian death is an easy death? Why do we believe that the hope for a life with Christ will make our death a gentle passage? A compassionate life is a life in which the suffering of others is deeply felt, and such a life may also make one's death an act of dying with others . . .

In Jesus' agony we see the agony of the world in all its gripping intensity: 'Sadness came over him, and great distress. Then he said: "My soul is sorrowful to the point of death" ' (Matthew 26:37). Is not every human being who wants to live with the mind of Christ also called to die with the mind of Christ? This can mean very different things for different people. It certainly does not have to mean the struggle Mother suffered. Yet it seems at least important to understand that those who live with Christ must also be prepared to die with him, to be willing even to accept the invitation to enter into his agony.

Death and faith

What then is this agony? Is it fear of God, fear of punishment, fear of the immensity of the divine presence? I do not know, but if I have any sense of what I saw, it was more profound. It was the fear of the great abyss which separates God from us, a distance which can only be bridged by faith. The test comes when everything that is dear to us slips away – our home and those we love, our body and its many ways of living, our mind and its caring thoughts – and there is absolutely nothing left to hold on to. It is then that one must have the faith to surrender to a loving Lord, to believe that he will not allow us to fall into a cruel and bottomless canyon, but will bring us to the safe home which he has prepared for us . . .

At the hour of death all becomes faith. Faith in God, who knows every fiber of our being and loves us in spite of our sins, is the narrow gate which connects this world with the next.

The prayers we said together became the place where we could be together without fear or apprehension. They became like a safe house in which we could dwell, communicating things to each other without having to grope for inadequate, self-made expressions. The Psalms, the Our Father, the Hail Mary, the Creed, the Litany of the Saints and many other prayers formed the walls of this new house, a safe structure in which we felt free to move closer to each other and to Mother, who needed our prayers in her lonely struggle.

Love and liberation

Yet the same love that reveals to us the absurdity of death also allows us to befriend death. The same love that forms the basis of our grief is also the basis of our hope; the same love that makes us cry out in pain also must enable us to develop a liberating intimacy with our own most basic brokenness. Without faith, this must sound like a contradiction. But our faith in him whose love overcame death and who rose from the grave on the third day converts this contradiction into a paradox, the most healing paradox of our existence.

Death indeed simplifies, death does not tolerate endless shadings and nuances. Death lays bare what really matters, and in this way becomes our judge.

I am constantly struck by the fact that those who are most detached from life, those who have learned through living that there is nothing and nobody in this life to cling to, are the really creative people. They are free to move constantly away from the familiar, safe places and can keep moving forward to new, unexplored areas of life ... I am thinking primarily of a spiritual process by which we can live our lives more freely than before, more open to God's guidance and more willing to respond when he speaks to our innermost selves.

Worry

To be *pre*occupied means to fill our time and place long before we are there . . . We say to ourselves, 'What if I get the flu? What if I lose my job? What if my child is not home on time? What if there is not enough food tomorrow? What if I am attacked? What if a war starts? What if the world comes to an end? What if . . . ?' . . . Much, if not most, of our suffering is connected with these preoccupations . . . They prevent us from feeling a real inner freedom. Since we are always preparing for eventualities, we seldom fully trust the moment . . . Our individual as well as communal lives are so deeply molded by our worries about tomorrow that today can hardly be experienced.

Our occupations and preoccupations fill our external and internal lives to the brim. They prevent the Spirit of God from breathing freely in us and thus renewing our lives.

Jesus responds to this condition . . . But his call to live a spiritual life can only be heard when we are willing honestly to confess our own homeless and worrying existence and recognize its fragmenting effect on our daily life. Only then can a desire for our true home develop. It is of this desire that Jesus speaks when he says, 'Do not worry . . . Set your hearts on his kingdom first . . . and all these other things will be given you as well' (Matthew 6:33).

The discipline of spirituality

The spiritual life is a gift. It is the gift of the Holy Spirit, who lifts us up into the kingdom of God's love. But to say that being lifted up into the kingdom of love is a divine gift does not mean that we wait passively until the gift is offered to us. Jesus tells us to set our hearts on the kingdom. Setting our hearts on something involves not only serious aspiration but also strong determination. A spiritual life requires human effort. The forces that keep pulling us back into a worry-filled life are far from easy to overcome.

Here we touch the question of discipline in the spiritual life. A spiritual life without discipline is impossible. Discipline is the other side of discipleship. The practice of a spiritual discipline makes us more sensitive to the small, gentle voice of God. The prophet Elijah did not encounter God in the mighty wind or in the earthquake or in the fire, but in the small voice . . .

Through a spiritual discipline we prevent the world from filling our lives to such an extent that there is no place left to listen. A spiritual discipline sets us free to pray or, to say it better, allows the Spirit of God to pray in us.

The discipline of solitude

In the beginning, solitude seems so contrary to our desires that we are constantly tempted to run away from it. One way of running away is daydreaming or simply falling asleep. But when we stick to our discipline, in the conviction that God is with us even when we do not yet hear him, we slowly discover that we do not want to miss our time alone with God. Although we do not experience much satisfaction in our solitude, we realize that a day without solitude is less 'spiritual' than a day with it.

The discipline of solitude . . . is a simple, though not easy, way to free us from the slavery of our occupations and preoccupations and to begin to hear the voice that makes all things new.

The discipline of solitude does not stand alone. It is intimately related to the discipline of community. Community as discipline is the effort to create a free and empty space among people where together we can practise true obedience. Through the discipline of community we prevent ourselves from clinging to each other in fear and loneliness, and clear free space to listen to the liberating voice of God.

The discipline of community

Friendship, marriage, family, religious life, and every other form of community is solitude greeting solitude, spirit speaking to spirit, and heart calling to heart ... Community has little to do with mutual compatibility. Similarities in educational background, psychological make-up, or social status can bring us together, but they can never be the basis for community. Community is grounded in God, who calls us together, and not in the attractiveness of people to each other. There are many groups that have been formed to protect their own interests, to defend their own status, or to promote their own causes, but none of these is a Christian community. Instead of breaking through the walls of fear and creating new space for God, they close themselves to real or imaginary intruders. The mystery of community is precisely that it embraces *all* people, whatever their individual differences may be, and allows them to live together as brothers and sisters of Christ and sons and daughters of his heavenly Father.

The discipline of community helps us to be silent together. This disciplined silence is not an embarrassing silence, but a silence in which together we pay attention to the Lord who calls us together. In this way we come to know each other not as people who cling anxiously to our self-constructed identity, but as people who are loved by the same God in a very intimate and unique way.

A *new hunger*

Through the discipline of solitude we discover space for God in our innermost being. Through the discipline of community we discover a place for God in our life together. Both disciplines belong together precisely because the space within us and the space among us are the same space.

The beginning of the spiritual life is often difficult not only because the powers which cause us to worry are so strong but also because the presence of God's Spirit seems barely noticeable. If, however, we are faithful to our disciplines, a new hunger will make itself known. This new hunger is the first sign of God's presence. When we remain attentive to this divine presence, we will be led always deeper into the Kingdom. There, to our joyful surprise, we will discover that all things are being made new.

Gifts and God's way

It is very naïve to think that our individual giftedness can be directly translated into a call. To say 'I can write well, so God wants me to be a writer; I can teach well, so God wants me to be a teacher; I can play the piano well, so God wants me to be a pianist,' makes us forget that our own self-understanding is not necessarily God's understanding of us. There was a time in which a one-sided view of humility led to the negation or denial of individual gifts. Hopefully, that time is gone. But to think that individual gifts are the manifestation of God's will reveals a one-sided view of vocation and obscures the fact that our talents can be as much the way to God as *in the way of* God.

In solitude we take some distance from the many opinions and ideas of our fellow human beings and become vulnerable to God. There we can listen carefully to him and distinguish between our desires and our task, between our urges and our vocation, between the cravings of our heart and the call of God.

Community in a secular age

... It is a sad development when retreats, days of recollection, or hours of meditation are simply left to the initiative of the individual. It is a sign of real maturity when the members of a community have a genuine desire to enter into solitude together and share regularly with each other the fruit of their prayers, meditations and studies. Being alone with God for yourself is a very different experience from being alone with God as part of your life together. I am deeply convinced that great renewal will develop wherever communities enter regularly into solitude to discover together where God is calling them. No important decision, no important change in direction should ever be made without periods of long, silent listening in which all members are participating in some way.

When we speak of our age as a secular age, we must first of all be willing to become aware of how deeply this secularism has entered into our own hearts ... In many of our religious communities God has become little more than the silver frame for our own pictures. Beautiful liturgies, insightful conferences and occasional retreats are considered very inspiring ... but somewhere – often deep down – we know that without them things would hardly be different. It is, therefore, not surprising that many people have left religious life rather easily ...

Secularism and solitude

The religious secularism that I have described has entered so deeply into our way of being in the world that it cannot be made subject to simple accusations. But it can be made subject to reflection, because it not only shows how closely we, as religious people, have become part of our emergency-oriented world, but it also explains why it has become difficult for our contemporary religious communities to be unambiguous witnesses to the living God.

It is in the context of this religious secularism that solitude receives its deepest meaning ... Solitude indeed is the place of the great encounter, from which all other encounters derive their meaning. In solitude, we meet God. In solitude, we leave behind our many activities, concerns, plans and projects, opinions and convictions, and enter into the presence of our loving God, naked, vulnerable, open and receptive. And there we see that he alone is God, that he alone is care, that he alone is forgiveness ... I am not saying this to suggest that there is an easy solution to our ambivalent relationship with God. Solitude is not a solution. It is a direction.

Discernment

Will we ever know whether we are living witnesses to the light or serving the prince of darkness? That is the question for the four priests who participated in the revolution in Nicaragua and are now members of the Sandinista cabinet. That, too, is the question for Christians active in agrarian reform, in the development of cooperatives for the *campesinos*, and in programs for better health and housing.

Christians are called to live in the world without being of it. But how do we know whether we are just in it, or also of it? My feeling is that all Christians who are serious about their vocation have to face this question at some point.

Discernment remains our lifelong task. I can see no other way for discernment than a life in the Spirit, a life of unceasing prayer and contemplation, a life of deep communion with the Spirit of God. Such a life will slowly develop in us an inner sensitivity, enabling us to distinguish between the law of the flesh and the law of the spirit. We certainly will make constant errors and seldom have the purity of heart required to make the right decisions. We may never know whether we are giving to Caesar what belongs to God. But when we continuously try to live in the Spirit, we at least shall be willing to confess our weakness and ask for forgiveness every time we find ourselves again in the service of Baal.

Learning Christ from the weak

This afternoon at three o'clock, my sister called from Holland to tell me that my sister-in-law had given birth to a daughter who was diagnosed as suffering from Down's syndrome. A week ago I wrote about having seen a Down's-syndrome child in the house of Pete Ruggere's neighbors; yesterday I read about that child in the *Wall Street Journal;* today I have a niece who suffers from the same disease . . . I still find it hard to appropriate this news. I cannot think about much else than this little child who will become the center of my brother and sister-in-law's lives and will bring them into a world of which they have never dreamt. It will be a world of new feelings, emotions and thoughts; a world of affections that come from places invisible in 'normal' people.

Laura is going to be important for all of us in the family. We have never had a 'weak' person among us. We all are hardworking, ambitious and successful people who seldom have had to experience powerlessness. Now Laura enters and tells us a totally new story, a story of weakness, brokenness, vulnerability and total dependency. Laura, who will always be a child, will teach us the way of Christ as no one will ever be able to do.

The fellowship of the weak

One of the most rewarding experiences of living in a strange land is the experience of being loved not for what we can do, but for who we are. When we become aware that our stuttering, failing, vulnerable selves are loved even when we hardly progress, we can let go of our compulsion to prove ourselves and be free to live with others in a fellowship of the weak. This is a true healing.

Ministry is entering with our human brokenness into communion with others and speaking a word of hope. This hope is not based on any power to solve the problems of those with whom we live, but on the love of God, which becomes visible when we let go of our fears of being out of control and enter into his presence in a shared confession of weakness.

This is a hard vocation. It goes against the grain of our need for self-affirmation, self-fulfillment and self-realization. It is a call to true humility.

The image of Christ

The more we come to depend on the images offered to us by those who try to distract us, entertain us, use us for their purposes, and make us conform to the demands of a consumer society, the easier it is for us to lose our identity. These imposed images actually make us into the world which they represent, a world of hatred, greed, manipulation and oppression. But when we believe that we are created in the image of God himself and come to realize that Christ came to let us reimagine this, then meditation and prayer can lead us to our true identity.

Latin America offers us the image of the suffering Christ. The poor we see every day, the stories about deportation, torture and murder we hear every day, and the undernourished children we touch every day, reveal to us the suffering Christ hidden within us. When we allow this image of the suffering Christ within us to grow into its full maturity, then ministry to the poor and oppressed becomes a real possibility; because then we can indeed hear, see and touch him within us as well as among us. This prayer becomes ministry and ministry becomes prayer. Once we have seen the suffering Christ within us, we will see him wherever we see people in pain. Once we have seen the suffering Christ among us, we will recognize him in our innermost self.

Fear

... Most of us people of the twentieth century live in the house of fear most of the time. It has become an obvious dwelling place, an acceptable basis on which we make our decisions and plan our lives. But why are we so terribly afraid? Why is it so hard to find fearless people? Would there be so much fear if it was not useful to somebody?

Fear is the great enemy of intimacy. Fear makes us run away from each other or cling to each other, but does not create true intimacy. When Jesus was arrested in the Garden of Gethsemane, the disciples were overcome by fear and they all 'deserted him and ran away' (Matthew 26:56)

God alone is free enough from wounds to offer us a fearless space. In and through God we can be faithful to each other: in friendship, marriage and community. This intimate bond with God, constantly nurtured by prayer, offers us a true home.

Intimacy

When we use the word 'intimacy' in our daily lives we easily associate it with privacy, smallness, cosiness and a certain exclusiveness. When someone refers to a conversation or a party as intimate we tend to think about a few people, a small space, or confidential subject matter. The word 'intimate' usually suggests the opposite of being open to the public.

. . . Our spiritual experience shows us something quite new. Those who have entered deeply into their hearts and found the intimate home where they encounter their Lord, come to the mysterious discovery that solidarity is the other side of intimacy. They come to the awareness that the intimacy of God's house excludes no one and includes everyone. They start to see that the home they have found in their innermost being is as wide as the whole of humanity.

It is of great importance to see the inner connection between intimacy and solidarity. If we fail to recognize this connection our spirituality will become either privatized or narrowly activist and will no longer reflect the full beauty of living in God's house.

Incarnation and solidarity

The mystery of the incarnation reveals to us the spiritual dimension of human solidarity. Because all humanity has been taken up into God through the incarnation of the Word, finding the heart of God means finding all the people of God. Therefore, a Christ in whom all people are not gathered together is not the true Christ. We who belong to Christ belong to all of humanity.

In our competitive world we are so used to thinking in terms of 'more' and 'less' that we cannot easily see how God can love all human beings with the same unlimited love while at the same time loving each one of them in a totally unique way.

But the spiritual life breaks through these distinctions ... The spiritual life allows us to experience that the same God who lovingly embraces all people has counted every hair of our heads (see Matthew 10:30) ...

The deeper our prayer becomes, the closer we come to this mystery of God's love. And the closer we are to this mystery the better we can live it out in our daily life. It frees us to appreciate other people's talents without being diminished by them and to lift up their uniqueness without feeling less unique ourselves. It allows us to celebrate the various ways of being human as a sign of the universal love of God.

Fear and fecundity

'Those who remain in me, with me in them, bear fruit in plenty' (John 15:5). With these words Jesus speaks about fruitfulness or fecundity. When Jesus himself and all humanity through him have become our true home, we can become truly fecund or fruitful people. The word 'fecundity' is not used often in daily conversation, but it is a word worth reclaiming, for it can put us in touch with our deepest human potential to bring forth life. That the word fecundity sounds archaic may indicate that the reality to which this word points is receding to the background of our consciousness in today's technological society.

Fear not only prevents intimacy; it also thwarts fecundity. When fear dominates our lives, we cannot quietly and patiently protect that holy space where fruit can grow.

I may have come to the theoretical insight that being is more important than doing, but when asked to just be with people who can do very little I realize how far I am from the realization of that insight. Thus, the handicapped have become my teachers, telling me in many different ways that productivity is something other than fecundity. Some of us might be productive and others not, but we are all called to bear fruit; fruitfulness is a true quality of love.

The vulnerability of God

The way of God is the way of weakness. The great news of the Gospel is precisely that God became small and vulnerable, and hence bore fruit among us. The most fruitful life ever lived is the life of Jesus, who did not cling to his divine power but became as we are (see Philippians 2:6–7). Jesus brought us new life in ultimate vulnerability . . .

It is in this extreme vulnerability that our salvation was won. The fruit of this poor and failing existence is eternal life for all who believe in him.

It is very hard for us to grasp even a little bit of the mystery of God's vulnerability. Yet, when we have eyes to see and ears to hear we can see it in many ways and in many places. We can see it when a child is born, the fruit of the love of two people who came together without defences and embraced each other in weakness. We can see it in the grateful smiles of poor people and in the warm affection of the handicapped. We can see it every time people ask forgiveness and are reconciled.

Learning from the poor

It is a tragedy of history that we have proved more eager to steal the material fruits of the labor of the poor than to receive the spiritual fruits of their lives.

We who live in the illusion of control and self-sufficiency must learn true joy, peace, forgiveness and love from our poor brothers and sisters. Martin Luther King, Jr, considered it just as important for the blacks in the United States to convert the whites as to gain equal rights. Likewise, it is as important for the rich to be converted by the poor as it is to share their wealth with the poor. As long as we only want to give and resist becoming receivers, we betray our desire to stay in control at all costs. Thus we remain in the house of fear.

How different would our world be if our main concern were to receive the fruits of the love of the poor and oppressed . . . What if we could see our southern neighbors first of all as people who pray with great devotion, who love their children and families deeply, who write lovely poems, and who have a spirit of joy and gratitude? Wouldn't we want to receive those gifts, we who have become too busy to pray, too lonely to keep our families together, too pragmatic for poetry, and too preoccupied with ourselves to be joyful or grateful?

Hope and the cross

In La Forestière, one of the L'Arche homes in France where deeply handicapped people live, I see how anguish sometimes finds expression in self-mutilation . . . It is hard to fathom what goes on in the hearts of such persons who have very limited ways of communicating; but just being with them leads me to suspect an existential fear, intense beyond our most compassionate understanding. The anxiety of these broken people gives us a glimpse of Jesus' agony in the Garden of Gethsemane . . . Their anxiety suggests an immense loneliness which nobody can penetrate, a homelessness that goes far beyond the need for a caring friend or a hospitable house, a rootlessness that opens up into chasms of human despair. The most one can do is to be present, not expecting any changes, but standing in loving awe at the immensity of human fear that Jesus came to carry with us to the cross and beyond.

In some mysterious way the handicapped and their assistants form a community of love, stronger than the agonies of its people. It is an expression of the divine presence in which both happiness and sadness are embraced as well as transcended. It has something to do with the cross, which has become for them a sign of hope. Somehow roots exist after all – roots beyond rootlessness.

Joy

Many people hardly believe anymore in the possibility of a truly joy-filled life. They have more or less accepted life as a prison and are grateful for every occasion that creates the illusion of the opposite: a cruise, a suspense novel, a sexual experience, or a few hours in a heightened state of consciousness. This is happiness in the house of fear, a happiness which is 'made in the world' and thus is neither lasting nor deeply satisfying.

The joy that Jesus offers his disciples is his own joy, which flows from his intimate communion with the One who sent him. It is a joy that does not separate happy days from sad days, successful moments from moments of failure, experiences of honor from experiences of dishonor, passion from resurrection. This joy is a divine gift that does not leave us during times of illness, poverty, oppression or persecution. It is present even when the world laughs or tortures, robs or maims, fights or kills. It is truly ecstatic, always moving us away from the house of fear into the house of love, and always proclaiming that death no longer has the final say, though its noise remain loud and its devastation visible. The joy of Jesus lifts up life to be celebrated.

Praying with icons

During a hard period of my life in which verbal prayer had become nearly impossible and during which mental and emotional fatigue had made me the easy victim of feelings of despair and fear, a long and quiet presence to this icon became the beginning of my healing. As I sat for long hours in front of Rublev's *Trinity*, I noticed how gradually my gaze became a prayer. This silent prayer slowly made my inner restlessness melt away and lifted me up into the circle of love, a circle that could not be broken by the powers of the world. Even as I moved away from the icon and became involved in the many tasks of everyday life, I felt as if I did not have to leave the holy place I had found and could dwell there whatever I did or wherever I went. I knew that the house of love I had entered has no boundaries and embraces everyone who wants to dwell there.

Within the circle of the Holy Trinity, all true knowledge descends into the heart. The Russian mystics describe prayer as descending with the mind into the heart and standing there in the presence of God. Prayer takes place where heart speaks to heart, that is, where the heart of God is united with the heart that prays. Thus knowing God becomes loving God, just as being known by God is being loved by God.

Sources and Index

The following books served as sources for this anthology. The abbreviations in parentheses which follow the titles are used in the index to indicate the sources, and page numbers in the sources, for the selected readings. The figures in bold type refer to the pages of readings in this book.

Behold the Beauty of the Lord: Praying with Icons *(BBL)*, Ave Maria Press, 1987

Clowning in Rome (CR), Doubleday, NY, 1979

Compassion (Com), Doubleday, NY, 1982

A Cry for Mercy (CFM), Doubleday, NY, 1981

The Genesee Diary (Gen), Doubleday, NY, 1981

¡Gracias! (Gr), Harper & Row, San Francisco, 1983

Lifesigns (L), Doubleday, NY, 1986

In Memoriam (IM), Ave Maria Press, Indiana, 1980

A Letter of Consolation (LC), Harper & Row, San Francisco, 1982

Love in a Fearful Land: A Guatemalan Story (LFL), Ave Maria Press, Indiana, 1985

Making All Things New (MATN), Harper & Row, San Francisco, 1981

The Way of the Heart (WHe), Harper & Row, San Francisco, 1981

With Open Hands (WOH), Ave Maria Press, Indiana, 1972

The Wounded Healer (WH), Doubleday, NY, 1979